CANNABIS REGENERATION

A MULTIPLE HARVEST METHOD FOR GREATER YIELDS

J. B. HAZE

GREEN CANDY PRESS

Cannabis Regeneration: A Multiple Harvest Method For Greater Yields

Published by Leabhar Inc., Toronto, Canada

Copyright © 2015 J.B. Haze
Photographs © 2015 J.B. Haze

ISBN 978-1-937866-04-4

Printed in China by Oceanic Graphic International

Sometimes Massively Distributed by P.G.W.

DEDICATION

For the island girl in the Beetle with the doobie

There are *three* paths: seed, clone, regeneration. Ignoring any one is akin to handing a third of the pie back to god.

—former two-timin' man

CONTENTS

ACKNOWLEDGEMENTS

I'd like to thank Andrew and the wonderful team (Heather, Ian and Jack) at Green Candy Press for their undying efforts to make this the very best book possible. From contract to culmination, it's been a joy.

JUST LIKE MAGIC

Over eight long and dutiful weeks you've flowered a sweet, succulent and fragrant plant. She's a keeper: 30 delicious colas, all glistening with goodness. However, just as you're holding pruning shears to her trunk, you're beating yourself up over having not taken clones or kept seeds.

"Damn…" you whisper under your breath, stumbling and stubbing your toe. "If I harvest her now she'll be gone forever—kaput! There's got to be a way to save these genetics without wasting all these yummy buds!"

Wiping the grimace from your face, and the blood from your foot, you carefully consider which of three possible actions to take:

1. Follow the instructions (in many a grow book) for attempting to "re-green" or "rejuvenate" the cannabis: Cut down your plant, leaving about 15 to 30% of the lower branches, foliage and buds behind. Flick the lights back to 24/0 (24 hours of light and none of darkness), cross your fingers and hope for the best.

2. Take mature age clones: Cut off the ripe buds, replanting them, following cloning protocol. Flick the lights back to 24/0, cross your fingers and hope for the best.

3. Utilize the Marijuana Regeneration System, as taught in this book: Harvest your entire plant, hanging her upside down to dry. Then initiate the regeneration of the remaining stump, growing out 60 or so new tips (each ready to begin flowering) over the next 38 days. All up, not bad for a plant that, prior to the chop, had just 30 colas.

Now, let's weigh the options:

Solutions 1 or 2? Forget 'em! I don't know about you, but I don't like putting in all that love and care, all those nutrients and lumens, only to sacrifice up to 30% of yield. Nor do I cherish lopping ripe buds for a possibly ill-fated cloning attempt when they could be put to better use; too much wasted goodness. There is no doubt that the first two methods may produce new growth—a good 50% chance, by my estimate. Yet the question is this: At what cost? In both instances, harvest is severely compromised (with corresponding reductions in yield) and you are left with a mutilated mess to dry.

Solution 3?

That's more like it. A full harvest to enjoy plus the potential to re-generate 60 new colas in the same pot. It's a no brainer. In fact, it's just like magic!

It may sound far-fetched, but the reality is anything but. This book is about refining existing wisdom and then applying it creatively. It offers a planned, tried and consistent technique; a reliable system allowing you to grow a single plant over and over again. Yummy. Decision made: Solution 3. Safe now to address the bloodied toe.

LIFE IS FULL OF SURPRISES

In the early 1980s I befriended my first real counter-culture hippie. He was a child of the 60s, growing up within a roach's throw of Haight Street. His attitude, artistic freedom and explorative mind impressed me no end. I was young, a little sheltered, still living at home and Ricky J wanted to introduce me to the wonders of the herb. Then, as now, it is a pleasure (some would say a duty) to mentor a friend in the canna-way.

"Mind-blowing, illuminating and life-changing," he teased before quietly cautioning, "The first time can be a little elusive; you may not notice anything." He gifted me two books in preparation for the journey. One for before (the hilarious parody of dope culture: *A Child's Garden of Grass* by Jack S. Margolis) and one for after (*The Hitchhiker's Guide to the Galaxy* by Douglas Adams).

I had, unknown to my good friend, also made a score of my own, and I'm not talking primo green here. Her name was Billie-Jean; a super-sweet, beaming island girl who just happened to be hosting at the Spanish cantina I was frequenting. As we sat in her beat-up V.W. Beetle around the corner from *Tokyo Jo's*, she reached into her over-sized hippie bag, pulling out a joint.

"Evva gotten high?" she asked—adding, almost immediately, "A little luvin' goes a long way!" Taken aback at the bizarre and coincidental turn of events, my rambling and confused attempt at explaining the *man-that's-weird* look on my face was cut short with the unintentional double entendre, "... are we going to do it, or what?" Unable to resist

the glow of her skin, the glitter of her blue, blue eyes and her moist shiny lips, I succumbed. But only after she quietly whispered, "Don't expect too much, it can be pretty subtle. You may not even notice."

Hmmm.

Following her instructions to the letter, the joint was properly lit. I was careful not to slobber, and received the relevant training on holding the toke and other breathing tricks. The car was bursting with smoke. But nothing. I felt nothing—apart from the titillation any young man should feel sharing a lipstick stained doobie with an incredible woman. Dinner was amazing. We settled in, bare feet entwined beneath the sunken table, enjoying the beautifully prepared teriyaki and *shabu shabu*. Dessert consisted of frozen ice cream—something that, I have to admit, never made sense to me. However, this evening the batter/crumb-work was marvelous; the way it partly crumbled, yet retained a shell-like formation that would, at times, slip gracefully along the gently curved arch of the spoon and then just hang. The little bubbles in the melting ice cream slid about with an amazing smoothness...

"You're high," she said.

The spoon made a little click on my teeth each time I passed it by my lips. I'd not noticed this before.

"You're high," she said again.

The music was simply wonderful and I don't think I'd before heard some of the instrumentation in what were familiar tunes.

"You're high," she said once more.

"Nah, no I am not," I purred back—quickly correcting myself as I looked up. The glimmer in this girl's eyes, the way the lighting in the room sparkled, and the surgically rendered mess of ice cream and crumbs convincing me. I had found the space. Or it had found me. Either way, it was wonderful.[1]

Many have reported the elusiveness of the initial "high" of marijuana, including famed astronomer and Pulitzer Prize winner Carl Sagan, who (writing as Mr. X[2]) in *Marihuana Reconsidered* (1971), said: "My initial experiences were entirely disappointing; there was no effect at all, and I began to entertain a variety of hypotheses about cannabis being a placebo..." Legendary cannabis activist and author of *The Emperor Wears No Clothes*, Jack Herer, tells a similar tale about his first experience.[3] If you ask around, those who remember the period between the 60s and 80s will relate similar stories.

Consider the same scenario—that is, introducing a newbie to the

joys of the herb—shifted to the current day. Could you, in all fairness (while rolling a joint of Chronic) declare to a friend, "... look mate, this is really subtle. You may not notice much at all." I think not. Today's cannabis seems—for the most part—a different experience to what it was decades ago.

Donning our retrospectacles, and peering at history, I think we can finger prohibition as the catalyst for this shift.

The 60s, 70s and early 80s were, undoubtedly, sativa-based times. Think "hippies, daisy-chains and Itchycoo Park" and you'll be recalling sativa days. The word "mellow" describes the period. Some of today's popular strains of cannabis sativa are Carnival, Yummy and Cotton Candy. The advertised names mirror the plant's qualities—gentle and fun. It has been said, "a good sativa is like slipping into a lovely warm bath."

On the other hand, today's most widely used variety, cannabis indica, produces an effect more readily felt in the body. The terms "body-hit," "one-toke-wonder" and "couch-lock" are often attributed to particularly potent strains of indica. Advertised names are also an indication of how hard these strains impact the end user. Would anyone expect anything gentle or subtle from plants labeled Kong, The Beast or Zombie Virus? None of these tally neatly with the *let's go sit in the sunshine, sing and make daisy chains* images of yesteryear's subtle highs.

So, why the shift?

Prohibition. As raids, busts and chemical defoliation became more of a risk in the last decades of the century, growers were forced indoors: The tall-growing sativa, with its long flowering time of between 12 and 20 weeks, simply became untenable. Ceilings were too low to accommodate such tall and leggy plants and the time between harvests was too long. Cannabis indica, on the other hand, is a small and squat plant that flowers in a very brief eight or so weeks and is easier to manage indoors.

Make no mistake, this shift indoors marked a turning point in our relationship with the species. It is this profound change that concerns us the most here. While I believe the segue from sativa to indica is alone sufficient to account for the oft-declared "cannabis is getting stronger" claim, it is the enforcement of controlled conditions, I feel, that has really made an impact on growing.

Moving indoors meant, for the first time, the farmer could control the exact parameters of the grow. Water, lighting and nutrients could be fine tuned to perfectly fit the plant's requirements. No longer was the crop at the mercy of the weather. Moving indoors forced the study of the photoperiod (how the length of the day affects growth patterns) in detail. It has led to better lights, refined nutrients, superior water delivery systems, consideration of the effects of humidity, temperature, root health and so much more. These intricacies were not well understood until the move indoors forced dedicated cultivators to do the research.

By understanding the details, we can better look after our plants. This allows them to reach further up towards the ceiling of potential. Due to the knowledge generated by being forced indoors, we are now growing better gardens.

Kicked off by prohibition, we have seen a revolution, not only in lighting efficiencies/technologies and the understanding of the plant's biology/behavior, but also in the tools and equipment required to grow successfully. Consider the vast array of grow tents, watering systems, clone propagation units, automated timers, CO_2 delivery systems and the like that are now available. Entire industries have grown from the new knowledge base. And grow books? Well, prior to prohibition, you could count them on the fingers of one hand. Nowadays there are dozens upon dozens of books dealing with the botany and wonder of the cannabis plant. How times have changed. The MRS itself has grown out of this new—ever-evolving—pool of information (and today's ease of access to the appropriate tools/supplies).

If you already know how to grow a great garden—potent and healthy—then transitioning to The MRS will be pain free and fun. For novices, I'd suggest you absorb as much information about growing cannabis as you can. I've included a basic reading list at the end of this book to start you on your way. You see, the better the grower you are, the better the results from The MRS will be. It is not a panacea to a successful grow; it is a pathway—allowing your existing skills to be expressed in an efficient, productive and potent manner.

You may never have believed that cannabis could regenerate once, let alone the two or more times that I intend to show you in this book. Well, as I said at the start of this introduction, life is full of surprises. And, as a girl called Billie-Jean once said, "… a little luvin' goes a long way!"

PART ONE

HOW IT WORKS

CONCEPTUALLY SPEAKING

THE MRS

INCREASED YIELD

SAVING LIGHT, POWER, SPACE AND CONSUMABLES

CHAPTER ONE

CONCEPTUALLY SPEAKING

Regeneration is a system for revegetating, re-flowering and re-budding a previously harvested plant—continuously.

The above statement is the very essence of this book and, for most, it will seem like a fairly ludicrous suggestion.

How can you possibly regenerate a plant to produce a second (or even third, or fourth or fifth...) harvest? When I say previously harvested, I really mean it: Nothing selective, no fancy pruning. We're talking about a chopped-at-the-trunk, hung upside down, old school harvest.

So then, what's the secret? What allows you to regrow what is essentially just a stump? Well, though on one hand it might seem crazy, on the other hand it's not so mystical after all. As already noted, regeneration is something known, published and—on occasion—used. However, the literature's scant coverage of the subject (and the sparse discussion of it on the internet) seems to have rendered it mostly invisible—to be pulled out of the hat (like the magic trick it is) only in an emergency. Through no fault of its own, regeneration has remained sidelined as a last ditch effort to save a dying plant.

I intend to prove to you that, on the contrary, regeneration can be so much more. My main argument in this book can be boiled down to two truths:

1. With familiarization of the regeneration technique (and a little practice) you can coax a single plant into delivering many consecutive harvests.

2. Each subsequent harvest has the potential to be superior to the one previous.

How exciting!

It may appear a little too reminiscent of Frankenstein's monster, this ability to regenerate. However, such strangeness (the pictured, double-ended bud, being an exception) does not extend to the treasures born and bred of regeneration.[1] The resulting flowers and buds are, in fact, healthy and indistinguishable in every way from those grown from seed or clone. The beautiful photographs gracing these pages are proof of the pudding. Note the growth sprouting from nodes, the lush green and healthy foliage—and dig the colors, form and density of the many buds. This is all good stuff, and it is all exactly as if grown from seed or clone—frosty, fragrant, plump and plentiful.

In addition, The Marijuana Regeneration System (MRS[2]), as explained in this book, allows you to increase the quality of your favorite plants. Flavor, potency, aroma and yield can be improved with each subsequent harvest cycle. I know this flies in the face of urban wisdom but all will be revealed with rational explanations and step-by-step instructions. In this book we shall learn that:

■ Regeneration can become the heart of a self-contained grow system, one with the potential for ongoing and incremental improvements in areas such as flavor, potency, aroma and yield.
■ Regeneration can be applied to produce enhanced results across all types of grow systems, big and small.
■ Regeneration can complement many areas of cultivation, including seed production, cloning and breeding.

So, get your Mary Shelley on; let's find out how it is possible to bring a plant back to life, regenerating her over and over. Allow me to introduce the star of our show, The MRS.

CHAPTER TWO

THE MRS

The Marijuana Regeneration System is offered not as a substitute for seed and clone growing, but as an additional technique—an extra arrow in your quiver. It's a nice pointy one too, presenting a sharp alternative to what's considered the norm.

The benefits of regeneration are especially bountiful for the hobby grower; the small-time guy (like me, and possibly you) growing one or two plants at a time for personal consumption. Medicinal growers, with strict plant limits, will also find The MRS a great way to maintain consistent supply and quality lineage. This is not to say that The MRS can't be expanded out to a multi-plant, multi-light monster grow. It undoubtedly can, and we'll discuss expanding the system later. But for now, let's keep it tight and focused on the small time cultivator.

Generally speaking, a grower like you or I does not want to deal with expensive lights, air filters, duct work, cloning stations (with their own specific lighting requirements), dozens of pots and bags of soil. Growing for the love of it (and to keep our heads in the right place), we like it easy, simple and cost-effective. This way we can love our ladies with total devotion—caressing the very best from them. And, under the umbrella of this intimate relationship, between grower and plant, The MRS really shines, delivering yield and quality from a tiny space.

The process of regeneration unfolds along a timeline like this:

1. The rescue, stabilization and initial regeneration of the donor plant (the just harvested plant—nothing more than a stump at this

point), which will take from four to 14 days. During this period new growth will magically spring forth.

2. A four to five week period of vigorous vegetation and training; the key to The MRS success. Note that this period is no longer than any normal vegetative one.

3. A regular eight to 10 week period for complete (and lush) flowering and budding.

As an overall growing discipline, regeneration offers multiple benefits, including:

■ High yield (60 to 100 colas per 12-inch (three and a half gallon) pot. (See Chapter 3)
■ The potential to increase yield and quality with each subsequent harvest. (See Chapter 4)
■ Minimal power usage (just a single, dedicated, low wattage light). (See Chapter 4)
■ Space and consumables efficiency (one pot, minimum grow medium and nutrients). (See Chapter 4)

That's all well and good—and it certainly sounds wonderful. But how do you do it? How do you infuse life into the scraggly, stump-like remains of your just harvested plant? The defined procedure for physically putting The MRS system to work will also be taught:

■ Tools and supplies needed to undertake regeneration. (See Chapter 5)
■ Rescue and stabilization of the plant. Post-harvest vascular management. (See Chapter 6)
■ Initial regrowth. (See Chapter 7)
■ Staking, teasing and training prior to re-flowering. (See Chapter 8)
■ Defoliation and maintenance prior to re-harvest. (See Chapter 9)
■ Doing it all over again, the next harvest. (See Chapter 10)

The above chapters cover the application of The MRS in a step-by-step manner, from cut to completion, with photographs detailing the plant's growth patterns. Taken together, all you need to fully implement The MRS (thus repeatedly regrowing the same plant) is covered.

The final chapters are a little different, stepping outside the clearly defined goals and aims of the original system. Here we learn how to adjust our procedures: Allowing continuous harvests and expanding The MRS into a multi-plant, multi-light behemoth capable of popping out buds by the thousands. We also explore combining regeneration with the established practices of cloning and controlled pollination (seed manufacture):

- The third harvest and beyond. (See Chapter 11)
- Cloning and pollinating with The MRS. (See Chapter 12)
- Expanding to grow multiple plants. (See Chapter 13)

Considering all that regeneration (The Mrs in particular) has to offer in the way of enhanced yield, cost-effective production and potent end product, I find it surprising that the approach has not become more widely known or exploited. My theory as to why this should be involves the evolution of the plant and this simple observation: Cannabis, since it first evolved (eons ago, in the carbon rich atmosphere it still desires), has *always* grown outdoors. Regeneration does not occur, in the cannabis plant, outdoors—it's simply not possible. Here's why: Outdoors, you are harvesting during the very short days—those with 12 hours of light or less. Regeneration, if it is to trigger, requires at least 18 hours of light per day (and preferably continuous light for consistent results). This sudden lengthening of the day does not occur naturally. You cannot reach up into the sky and halt dear old Sol's movements, elongating the daylight hours. In fact, the photoperiod can only be manipulated to achieve an instantly stretched day *indoors*. And, it's only very, very recently in the cannabis plant's evolution that she's encountered indoor lighting.

Could this fact, that regeneration is not encountered outside, be the reason the concept has remained *sub rosa*? Whatever the answer, I am convinced that now is the time for regeneration to come out of the proverbial closet; to shine, and to take its place in grow rooms across the world. The MRS is a friendly and easy way to achieve this dream.

CHAPTER THREE

INCREASED YIELD

The MRS has transcended both growing from seed and cloning to become my preferred day-to-day method of cultivation. Nowadays I find myself treating a plant grown from seed as a precursor for an intended regeneration.

My prior decades of sporadic cultivation were spent with traditional techniques, both indoor and outdoor; seeds, clones, indica, sativa, wet climates and dry. And, as any grower who has worked with plants over stretches of time will tell you, sometimes the girls will do strange things.[1] Odd stuff—quirks like having a simple topping result in five or six new shoots, or having a plant suddenly turn purple.

One peculiarity teased me over the years, eventually becoming the catalyst for The MRS. I had observed that certain plants, even those harvested right down to a stump, would, just sometimes, spontaneously burst into new growth. While this occurrence was occasional, it was always surprising: Life springing from a mere nub and a few straggling calyxes. I began considering this new growth as a possibility for systematic adaption, and thinking *How can this amazing will to grow be utilized?* I soon started to look into how best to ensure the magical regeneration every time, and how to maximize the plant's zest for rapid proliferation.

I now always consider the initial grow of a plant (from seed) as a precursor to regeneration. During this initial grow, the aim is fine-tuning such things as nutrient intake (is the plant receiving enough, too much, is she wilting or browning at the tips?), disease and pest

3.1 A just harvested stump, ready to be rescued and regenerated.

control (have pests been detected and treated, are there signs of disease?), deficiencies (have nitrogen, manganese and other irregularities been noted and addressed?) and so on. These, and any other possible problems along the way, create stress. When the plant has to deal with such headaches, she can't excel.

Identifying and then avoiding the pests, disease, deficiencies, watering problems and the like, encountered the first time around, creates a stress-reduced second grow. A close relationship between plant and grower, with the plant's needs being tended to precisely and with great passion, will assure a bountiful harvest.

We can see the rapid growth of a regenerated plant for ourselves—just look at **photographs 3.1** and **3.2**. The first photograph shows the potted remains of a just harvested plant. It's nothing more than a nub of stump with a couple of scraggly buds. This stump was saved, regenerated and then vegetated over six weeks, quickly reaching the mad flurry of healthy growth shown in the second photograph. Gob smacking; faster than both seed and clone, in fact. What's equally impressive, I think, is that she was grown with a single 36-watt light and two hours of sun, twice a week, during watering/feeding sessions.

3.2 The same stump, five weeks later, full of vigorous growth and potential budding sites.

Such vigorous growth is a hallmark of The MRS and is especially beneficial for the personal grower with only a plant or two in the grow room. Under such circumstances, sufficient yield is about having enough high quality head-stash (or medicine) until the next plant is ready. To lay in a solid supply cost-effectively, with a single light and one pot is advantageous and requires special attention to plant selection and vegetative technique. We must maximize potential, squeezing as much goodness from the plant as we can. We must push her towards the built-in, genetically encoded limit for the production of flowers, resin, potency and aroma. Called the ceiling of potential, this is the very maximum a plant can deliver. Once the ceiling is reached, nothing will produce further yield or quality.

Typically, a plant will only approach its threshold if grown outdoors, in the ultimate conditions, where, depending on its heritage, it may max out as a huge 15- to 20-foot giant. The same plant, grown indoors, will be an eighth of this size (or way, way less), thus never approaching its maximum yield. To comprehend this is to understand how, when growing indoors, there's always plenty of extra yield to be

3.3 Good quality LED grow light illuminates a pot abundant in bud.

squeezed from the plant. You are always reaching for the elusive ceiling of potential.

The regenerative secret to maximizing yield indoors is dependent upon training: Creating a plant/light interface designed to pull maximum yield from a single, and cost-effective, light source. **Photograph 3.3**.

To better understand the idea of interfacing the plant and light source to maximize growth, consider how a cannabis plant (if left to grow naturally) will form the familiar Christmas tree shape. **Figure 1**. Indoors, grown under a single light, only the apex (top one third of the plant) will receive sufficient illumination for vigorous growth. This is due to the throw exhibited by the light; usually about 18 to 24 inches of usable lumens. Colas forming down the sides of the plant, and at the bottom, will not grow as plump as they could. They're simply not receiving sufficient light. This type of growth pattern can be seen in many of the photographs in glossy books and magazines. Indoor lighting, via its static overhead nature, encourages this type of floral expression.

Plants that are grown outdoors get a better deal. The daily motion

Figure 1. Grown indoors, a traditional Christmas tree-shaped plant only receives light at its apex.

Figure 2. Grown outdoors, the movement of the sun across the sky illuminates the whole plant.

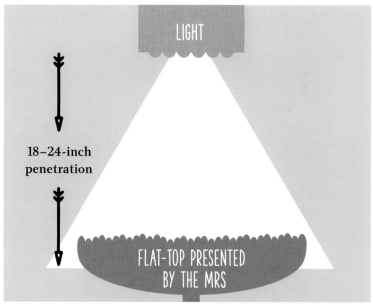

Figure 3. A plant, trained with a flat top, interfaces well with a single light. This is the heart of The MRS.

3.4 Plant trained to exhibit a flat top for optimum light interface.

3.5 A sweet, medium-sized bud, typical of The MRS way of growing.

of the sun (its movement from East to West across the sky) ensures that the entire plant receives the energy required for vigorous growth. **Figure 2**. Outdoors, it is possible to grow huge plants—bushes the size of small cars.

However, setting up a rig to move a light, simulating the sun's motion indoors, is impractical for our modest purposes. Fortunately, there is a cost-effective and easy answer: We can train the regenerating plant so she better interfaces with a single light source. This is done by arranging all the colas on the top of the plant, all within the available lumen hot zone. I will teach a technique using small stakes that simulates a SOG or SCROG set-up, resulting in a plant with a completely flat top.[2] As you can see in **figure 3**, the plan is to arrange all the growing colas to receive an equal portion of light. **Photograph 3.4** is a real plant, with a real flat top. The outer buds will receive a little extra light due to reflection, and they'll grow a little taller and plumper due to this. It's an effect I call cratering, and we'll learn how to deal with it later. Typically, the buds grown with The MRS are a consistent medium size—best for even drying, and preferable for slow curing. **Photograph 3.5**.

Buds climbing from our pots, like armies of obese clowns, is one of regeneration's marvels; something that must be seen to be believed. This marathon of vigor takes one of two forms—either elongation or flurry.

ELONGATION

This begins four to 10 days after rescue, with the saved bud exhibiting signs of new and bright green leaf matter. Over the days, this new growth will elongate—the entire bud stretching out, following it. The bud is reverting to a single growing tip. As it reaches for the light, the old bud material spreads out along the branch. In due course, this growing branch can be pinched out (or tipped), encouraging it to split into two growing shoots.

FLURRY

Truly a magical thing to behold, this is nature at her most impressive. After about four to 10 days from rescue you will notice some bright green growth barely peeking through the older material. It will be quite vivid, contrasting against the surrounding, dying-off bud material. Then, after a few more days, you'll witness some of the old and seedless pods (up to a dozen of them) developing stalks and pushing skyward.

What's so amazing about the flurry, apart from the benefit of so many growing tips sprouting from a single bud, is the magical manner in which the calyxes transform back into growing shoots. Remember, up until harvest (just a week or so ago) these were ovaries in waiting, each with two pistils (white flowers). Now, as if by magic, they are reverting to leaf matter. The photographs in the following gallery show this metamorphosis in Attenborough-style detail.

The flurry is another of the attributes making regeneration so attractive. You are so well ahead of a typical seed grow which, at seven to 13 days, will present only one growing tip. Two buds, flurried, offer six to 12 growing tips over the same time period. All things considered, it should be obvious that a flurried bud is superior to a germinated seed at two weeks. A flurried bud is also superior to an elongated bud. There is a way to encourage flurry, and it will be taught later, in Chapter Six.

Flurry is also an essential part of understanding how we can achieve great yields from a small pot and a single light. It is the foundation upon which we shall build our flat top—maximizing the surface area presented to our light source. As well, we put the plant's fervor for growth to full use. The cannabis plant always grows towards the light. She'll grow pretty much left, right, sideways, in a spiral and even horizontally in order to reach it. As it turns out, horizontal growth has very clear advantages when it comes to bud formation (and flat top creation). We'll put the plant's love of growing and desire for light to good use as we train each of the flurried tips into between six and eight buds-to-be. If you do the math, that's going to easily exceed our expectations.

By ensuring a flat top, for maximum light absorption, we can fill out a 12-inch pot with between 60 and 100 budding sites, all during the course of a typical five to seven week vegetative period. The resulting canopy will be champing at the bit to go floral.

The magic of regeneration—new, bright green growth, peering through dense bud, reaching for the light. Calyxes, which only a week or two ago awaited fertilization, develop stalks pushing them skyward. New growth unfurls, twisting and turning: Rebirth.

CHAPTER FOUR

SAVING LIGHT, POWER, SPACE & CONSUMABLES

POWER

Lighting is one of the key areas of development that has been forced along by prohibition's callused hand. The effective indoor production of cannabis depends squarely upon excellent and power-efficient lighting. While the hardware has become more effective at delivering the lumens (units of light), the rising cost of electricity has become an international problem. In some parts of the world it is now cheaper to buy an ounce of dank cannabis on the streets for less than it costs in electricity to grow the equivalent at home.

For the small time grower, who wants little impact on his electricity account, traditional grow lights, typically drawing hundreds of watts, become problematic. Not only is there the huge power bill to consider, but such lighting also creates heat. This must be vented away from the grow area, often requiring additional power to run fans. More hassles, more expense. Technology is evolving to address these concerns and it's a far wider consideration than cannabis cultivation.

LIGHT

We are fortunate, in this respect, to be living in the times we do. Twenty years ago we had neither the understanding nor the technology to address the need for efficient, tuned lighting. To explain the idea of tuned lighting, let's examine why our plants look green. Sounds like a silly question, and the easy answer is chlorophyll, right?

Yes, that's true. But, why do the plants look green? It's because the light, reflected off the plant, consists of the frequencies making up green. In other words, the parts of the spectrum combining to make the green we see, is not used by the plant: It's rejected, reflected, wasted—which is why you see it.

This is where the new breed of grow light, the LED (Light Emitting Diode), with specific plant-friendly output, saves the day. These lights are extremely efficient because they don't waste energy creating undesired frequencies not required by the plant's photosynthetic processes. Ever noticed the lack of green in photographs taken of a plant under an active LED light? That's because there is no reflection of unwanted (green) light, **photograph 4.1**. With traditional lighting

4.1 Under the illumination of a tuned LED grow light, the green leaves of the plant appear almost black.

4.2 Hydro Grow lights: 21X-Pro (36-watt) and 84X-Pro (145-watt).

you are paying to generate this unwanted spectra, and you'll see it reflected (pardon the pun) on your power bill.

LED grow lights use a tuned mix of frequencies, avoiding the unwanted bits. The special mix of red, orange and blue frequencies give your plants all they need. You also benefit by not having to deal with the dissipation of heat.

The future of Horizontal Farming, both for food production on a grand scale, and for us, the humble cannabis cultivator, is not just dependent on the cost-effectiveness of the LED lights; it's rooted in the tuned spectral frequency these lights can offer. Many claims have been made, and will continue to be made, by manufacturers touting the latest magic light. A good rule of thumb is this: a great light is not a cheap light. Do your research.

4.3 A good light, like this Hydro Grow 21X-Pro (36-watt) features both a sturdy hanging fixture, and handy power-through capability, allowing other lights to be daisy-chained to it.

I use and recommend Hydro Grow lights, specifically the models 21X-Pro (36w) and 84X-Pro (145w) as shown in **photograph 4.2**. All the photographs in this book are of plants grown under either/both of these lights.[1]

Find a good LED light, one specifically tuned for plant growth. It will cost-effectively vegetate and flower your plants with vigor for years. You'll hardly notice it on your power bill, and neither will the power company. Be sure the light you choose has a proper and sturdy fixing for safe hanging, like the unit shown in **photograph 4.3**. A power-through feature, allowing further lights to be daisy-chained off the first, is also a handy.

LED grow lights throw quite a defined beam, the smaller units being perfect for lighting a single 12-inch pot.

4.4 Tucked into the corner of a dark room, a 12-inch pot full of buds, flourishes under the illumination of a small LED grow light.

SPACE

The benefits of growing one high-yielding pot beneath one high-efficiency light in order to produce a superior yield cannot be overstated. These are major benefits, as are the savings to be made on physical space and consumables.

Space saving is immediate and obvious. One pot, one light: Simple. The entire rig—both pot and light—can be tucked away in the corner of a dark room, **photograph 4.4**. The configuration could even be as simple as hanging the light over the back of a chair, illuminating the pot on the floor. Whatever you do, be sure to only use the light as is intended by the manufacturer. In other words, don't hang a light that is not designed to be hung. Of course, it is preferable to have better control over the environs, so a dedicated grow cabinet (small cupboard) is the ideal. If you already have a suitable grow room, cabinet or the like, then you are ready to proceed. Gear-wise, The MRS requires nothing more of you.

 CONSUMABLES

Consumables are saved because you can complete both the initial grow and then the first regeneration in the same pot. No need to swap out soil or other grow medium. It is also possible to regenerate for the second time: A third harvest. Any further harvests will require up-sizing as the roots will be frantic for room. Three harvests? You could pull close to three hundred colas from that. All from one pot, all on 12 square inches of floor space. Traditionally, producing so many buds would require additional growing pots, specific cloning pots and lights, extra grow medium, nutrients and the like. Then, there's the physical workload—dealing with all that extra baggage. The MRS makes it so much easier.

In many ways the concept of regeneration appears Tardis-like—producing way more than expected from a small space.[2] As a grow system it can reap benefits far greater than expected.

CHAPTER FIVE

PREPARATION

Regeneration both begins and ends at the same point—trunk-side, pruning shears in hand.

You may be feeling a little apprehension at this point. It's okay; the idea of bringing a plant back to life is pretty strange. We have new things to learn, new techniques to master. Recall that none of this is dabbling in the black arts or anything very mysterious. It's just good gardening technique. So, don't fret in any way; no magical powers are required, and I'm going to walk you through the whole process, one step at a time.

Although, as we've already discussed, it is possible to regenerate a cannabis plant several times, I'm going to assume that this is your first regeneration, and so I'll pick up your grow just before your first harvest. Successive harvests require a slightly different approach; but first things first.

I'll assume you've grown your plant from seed, and she's bursting with bud and ready to be chopped. So let's run through the method, and then we'll set about putting our theory into practice.

 THE METHOD

The Harvest: It's a brutal moment in your plant's life—being severed at the ankles and then hung upside down to dehydrate. Nasty; almost medieval. But this very traditional practice of hanging an entire

5.1 *Training a growing tip into a horizontal growth path.*

plant—*in toto*—permits moderated dehydration, allowing chlorophyll to be thoroughly dissipated. Slow drying is the gateway to fine tasting and aromatic herb.

The MRS accommodates this: You are permitted to chop and hang the entire plant, leaving only the lowermost one or two buds. Repeat: Just one or two buds, that's all you leave behind for the future regeneration. No leaving behind the lower branches, no leaving behind a quarter of your juicy buds and no other foliage considerations. Harvest, to all practical intents and purposes, is a normal one: Chop and hang. From this moment, though, we will move into fresh territory.

The Rescue: Immediately after the donor plant has been chopped, and everything above the cut hung upside down to dry, the resulting stump (with its remaining bud or two) must be stabilized with urgency. We will save her before she begins to die.

The Regrowth: Following the successful rescue and stabilization of the plant, she'll be out of the IC Unit and in full recovery. We will now begin the process of encouraging regrowth. Both elongating buds and

5.2 Adjusting a stake to maintain the flat top canopy.

flurrying buds will be staked out into a horizontal growth pattern aimed at the outer rim of the pot. We'll employ wooden skewers with bendy wire hooks to do this. These allow the plant to be trained in a natural way, at *her leisure*—along the paths best suited to her growth patterns, **photograph 5.1**.

The Rapid Growth Phase: The benefits of following the plant with the stakes is that new sprouting shoots—along the horizontally growing branches—will be fully exposed to both you and the light source. If you can see the new shoots, so can your light. You'll be able to further tease them out during development—something not possible if they were trapped beneath a SCROG screen. The real benefit of the staking approach is the ability to adjust the height of individual buds on the fly, **photograph 5.2**. You are maintaining the *flat top*—ensuring consistency and efficiency.

The Second Harvest: At this point, having nurtured the plant through a regular flowering and budding period, we find ourselves back at the beginning—or rounding the circle, if you will. Just as we began with a plant ready to harvest, so we find ourselves back at this point. However, this is not the end; you can, if you wish, prep the plant for a third cycle, and a fourth, and even more. I'll discuss this later in the book.

 ## TOOLS AND SUPPLIES

The tools and supplies needed to rescue, stabilize, encourage and develop growth (including the desired flat top) are shown in **photograph 5.3**. They are:

- Pruning shears, scissor or garden cutters: Needed to cut the plant at trunk for harvest. Should be sharp for a clean cut.
- Duct tape: Used to create an airtight cap (or seal) for the donor plant's exposed portion of trunk.
- Kitchen skewers: Made of bamboo and often available in two sizes (thick and thin), these will be used as stakes to pin down growing tips into horizontal growth trails.
- Twist-ties or gardening wire: To be affixed to non-pointy ends of skewers—making bendable hooks that can secure growing branches.
- Hot glue gun: Used to permanently bond the twist-ties or gardening wire to the skewers.

5.3 Tools and supplies required to implement The MRS.

Your total outlay for the above should not be any more than a few dollars, unless you need to buy the glue gun, then it will be a few more. Everything will be found at your hardware or gardening store, except the skewers. These you'll find in the supermarket as they're normally used for skewering meat and vegetables.

🌱 MAKING THE MRS STAKES

If you find yourself with a little time on your hands before your harvest, get yourself settled in and make your MRS stakes long before you need them. These are best made in batches of 100. Handy, as the skewers normally come in such packs. Same with the twist-ties. During the rapid growth phase you'll be constantly reaching for one of these stakes, so it's prudent to have a good stash (isn't it always?). If possible, I prefer to use plastic coated garden wire over the twist-ties. It's rugged and better to work with, lasting long after the twist-ties begin to weaken.

100 stakes will take about one CD's worth of listening time to manufacture. So chill and spin your favorite album (or choose a playlist on your portable device).

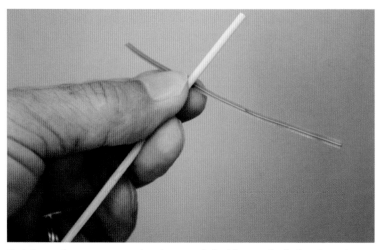

5.4 Preparing to wrap a twist-tie around the blunt end of a bamboo skewer.

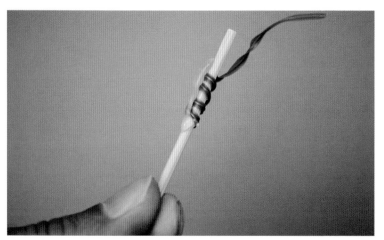

5.5 The twist-tie is bonded to the stake with a squirt from a hot glue gun.

1. Preheat the glue gun.

2. Place 100 skewers and 100 twist-ties on the table in front of you. (If using gardening wire, precut a hundred 3-inch lengths.)

3. Take a tie in your right hand, holding it to the blunt end of a skewer held in your left hand. Pin one end of the tie to the skewer with your left thumb as shown in photograph 8.2. Twist this around the skewer three or four times and then secure with a glob of hot glue photograph 8.3. This will prevent the tie from pulling free during

5.6 *A batch of The MRS stakes, ready to be put to work.*

enthusiastic growth. Place this skewer aside, with the hot end over-hanging the table, allowing the glue to cool and set.

4. Repeat 99 times. When finished, gather all the stakes in an ordered bunch and secure with a broad elastic band. **Photograph 5.6.** You'll be able to pull one free, from the wiry end, as required.

5. Turn both the hot glue gun and the CD player off.

Throughout, be careful not to become overly distracted by your music. Remember: The hot glue gun is hot, and the stakes (with their wiry bits) are pointy.

THE CROSSOVER HARVEST

The moment of harvest, in preparation for our first regeneration, is upon us. This is a special moment, the crossover harvest. It's the only time the plant will be harvested as one grown from seed (or clone). From now, she'll cross over to the realm of regeneration: All future harvests to be borne of this, not seed.

The plant you have lovingly grown to full maturity is sitting before you. Her buds glisten and the room smells divine. She will have been flushed and allowed to dry out just a little. These are measures that you've taken prior to harvest—cleansing the plant of nutrient signatures and allowing chlorophyll to begin breaking down. It's traditional

5.7 Very low on the trunk–a perfect pair of buds, allowing for a complete and traditional harvest of the whole plant above.

preparation for drying and curing good clean-burning, and sweet-tasting, herb. Proceed with the harvest as follows:

1. Ensure that your scissor or garden cutters are capable of cutting through the trunk with one jagged-free cutcut.

2. Sterilize the cutters. Unlike a traditional harvest, regeneration requires a clean and healthy cut. A solution of 10% bleach (or hydrogen peroxide) in water is ideal for sterilization. Soak your cutters for a few minutes, then rinse. Alternately, wipe the blades using a rag damped with methylated spirits. Vodka or any spirit may be substituted. A cheap aftershave (it's the alcoholic content that makes your face zing) or a disinfectant hand-wipe will also do the trick. Be sure to dry the cutters completely before use.

3. Locate a spot an inch or so above the lowest one or two buds on the main trunk. **Photographs 5.7 and 5.8** show perfect huddles—very low on the trunk—allowing for a complete and traditional harvest of the whole plant above. The regular house key, jammed into the grow medium in the latter photograph, indicates scale—demon-

5.8 A key, jammed into the grow medium, indicates scale—demonstrating how little bud matter is required for regeneration.

strating how little bud matter needs to be retained for regeneration.

4. Holding the cutters horizontally, cut the trunk at the position located. Do not cut on an angle—as you do with cloning (to increase surface area)—but straight across. You want the area exposed by the cut to be as small as possible: A circular cross-section has a smaller surface area than an oval one.

5. Hang the top 99% of the plant upside down to begin the drying process.

6. Immediately return to the potted trunk and begin the rescue/stabilization routine, described in the following chapter. Time is of essence here. Don't become distracted by the harvested material, removing fan leaves and other tidying up. These things can wait until later.

So far, so good. You are already a step ahead of where you would normally find yourself. This makes you a forward thinking person. It also makes you someone with a full, lush, no compromise harvest and the potential to regenerate a repeat performance. You are ready to start the real process: Bringing your plant back to life.

CHAPTER SIX

RESCUING AND REGENERATING YOUR HARVEST PLANT

Within ten minutes of making the chop, you'll want to cap the wound and then promptly address other issues like nutrients and the light cycle. The aim is to immediately reduce stress. To put it into perspective, imagine if your body had been completely severed at the ankles: You'd be stressed, seriously stressed. Now, consider how your feet would feel about it! Here are the three steps you must follow:

 STEP ONE: CAPPING THE DONOR PLANT

Consider the duct tape a medicinal plaster. What you need to do is seal off the stump's open wound—partly in an effort to stabilize the plant's plumbing, which is well and truly shot, but also to protect the exposed innards from air, light, dirt, insects and bacteria. Fortunately, the target buds that we'll be working with are below the cut point, and are thus serviced by the plant's vascular system before the damage is encountered.[1] However, we do not want air to sink into the wound, down to where the buds are serviced—creating a usually fatal embolism (air pocket). Seal off the wound immediately with duct tape as follows:

1. Eyeball the cut on the trunk, estimating the wound's diameter. Let's assume it's half an inch.
2. Tear off a square piece of duct tape twice the estimated diameter. So, for this example, that's a one-inch square piece of tape.
3. Center the tape (adhesive side down) across the wound. Now,

6.1 Square of duct tape positioned to seal the severed trunk.

6.2 Folding and squeezing the tape around the trunk.

6.3 *Wrapping a second piece of tape around the first.*

6.4 *The tape now encircling the trunk, creating an airtight cap.*

with thumb and fingers, secure the tape, pressing it firmly down around the edges, photographs 6.1 and 6.2.

4. Tear off a second piece of tape, the same width as the first, but long enough to encircle the trunk. Wrap it around the trunk, securing the first piece in position, photographs 6.3 and 6.4. Be thorough—make this as airtight as possible. Squeeze it tight.

Now that your plant is capped, the urgency is eased. She'll be a little thirsty, so we now need to feed her some water and prepare her with a mild bed of nutrients.

⬡ STEP TWO: NUTRIENTS

Not only is it traditional practice to allow the growing medium to dry a little prior to harvest, good technique also demands that the plant be flushed for a couple of weeks prior. This flushing—pouring a large quantity of water through the pot—is designed to flush or rinse out remaining nutrients that would otherwise taint the final product. Several flushes, across the final two weeks of flowering, normally do the trick, giving a nice clean product. However, it does rinse the goodness out of the grow medium. If we are to regenerate our plant, she will require nutrients at some point. We need to make sure these are available for when she is ready.

■ Fill a small watering can with tepid (lukewarm) water. Remember, we are trying to reduce stress as much as possible. The shock of cold water is not welcome at this point.

■ Balance the pH to your norm. (The ideal balance, best suited to the particular strain you are growing, will have been established during the first grow—prior to the initial harvest. Both strain and grow medium dictate the pH requirements. You'll be between 5.8 and 6.8 as a rule. I grow in 100% perlite and hold my pH at 6.0. I believe this to be very important for the delicate beginnings of regeneration).

■ Mix in a mild (25%) solution of your regular vegetative nutrient. This should contain nitrogen and the other nutrients that your plant will need when she begins to sprout new growing shoots. Be careful. Many fertilizers are hot, and should be considered full strength at 50%. So take it easy. You want a mild solution, one similar to what you'd use when transplanting, repotting or at other

6.5 A pair of buds about to receive a minor hair cut.

6.6 The top one third trimmed from each bud.

6.7 Our just rescued plant following her hair cut.

stressful moments in a plant's life. We require a firm but gentle dose of nitrogen, and the availability of other essentials like Phosphorus, Potassium, Calcium, Sulphur, Iron and Magnesium. I use a 25% solution of either *CANNA Vega,* which is a Dutch grow formula, or *Power-Feed For Veggies* (made by *Seasol International Pty Ltd*). This is an organic fertilizer containing a nice spectrum of base elements, amino acids and a high level of nitrogen. I combine this with a 25% dilution of a product called *Seasol.* Made by the same company, this is a seaweed extract containing no nitrogen, but an abundance of other trace goodies. You want to make sure that your plant has all the nutrients she needs to recover strongly, but you don't won't to overpower her. As with any grow, you will increase the strength of your nutrients *after* your plant has found her feet and entered a phase of abundant growth.

■ Check the pH making sure it's still stable. If not, adjust accordingly. We cannot afford pH problems at this point.

■ Water the capped plant heavily so that the roots are saturated and run-off is observed at the bottom of the pot.

■ Set the watered pot on a little wedge, or a gentle slope, enabling excess water to run free. (A small pebble will do the trick). Allow 20 minutes for this. You do not want the pot to remain saturated. Cannabis does not like wet feet.

Earlier, when discussing the two differing types of regrowth we can expect—elongation or flurry—I mentioned tipping the scales towards the preferred flurry. To do this, we give the buds a little haircut. Using a sharp and sterilized pair of scissors, trim one third off the top of each of the soon-to-be-regenerating buds. **Photographs 6.5** and **6.6** show a pair of buds before and after a haircut. This mild surgery has the effect of taking out the growing tip and discouraging elongation. And, much like when you tip a terminal shoot on a vegetating plant, energy is relocated to the growing areas immediately below. In our case, energy is shifted to the surrounding calyxes. It is the transformation of the calyxes back into growing tips that creates the flurry we desire. **Photograph 6.7** is our just rescued plant following her mild haircut.

At this point, your plant is about as comfortable as she's going to get. To encourage regrowth, we simply need to adjust the lighting regime—forcing immediate and rigorous photosynthesis.

⬡ STEP THREE: THE LIGHTING REQUIREMENTS

The regeneration process is kickstarted by placing the plant back into a vegetative lighting schedule. You will have previously flowered the donor plant with a 12/12 (12 hours with lights on and 12 with lights off) regime. Regeneration will require 24/0. I'm usually not a fan of continuous illumination, as I believe a plant needs its night cycle. However, to kickstart the plant into regenerative mode you must not allow her to sleep, not for a moment. So 24-hour illumination it is. (I change to 20/4 after new growth has become apparent.)

Another important consideration is light intensity. Your plant has everything it needs to move on: An established root system, nutrients, water and now light. Unlike cloning—which requires a gentle light to moderate photosynthesis, allowing for initial root development—our aim is to force photosynthesis immediately. Thus the intensity of the light source is of importance. Being careful not to burn the plant, lower your light for maximum brightness and lumen-saturation. Because our plant already has an established root system, she's ready to get down and dirty.

6.8 The same plant two weeks into regeneration, the trimmed buds flurrying.

While the lighting requirements for kicking off regeneration are the opposite of what's desired for cloning, the necessity for peace and rest is similar. It is now important to leave the plant alone, allowing her to recover without disturbance. The leaves are like solar panels, and an about-to-be-regenerated plant cannot spare energy needlessly reconfiguring them to face the light if moved. My golden rule here is to walk away for three days. Then, after this time, I'll check to see if she needs a watering. If so, she is watered with tepid pH adjusted water. In another two (to four) days you should see signs of regrowth—revealing itself as new leaf formation at the crown of the buds, or as a couple of the calyxes being pushed upwards on tiny stalks.

Once you see these first signs of regrowth you will know regeneration has been successful. If you see no signs of new growth after a week or ten days, be patient. Give her another week. Strains with high vigor are always the best to regenerate—F1 hybrids (the immediate offspring of parents consisting of two different strains) being astounding in this respect. However, some slower plants may take two solid weeks to show signs of regrowth.

A plant that has not revealed any signs of new life after three weeks should be discarded. Such a plant does not have the vigor we desire for energetic regeneration. No such problems with our rescued lady. The flurrying buds, two weeks out, are the signs of a successfully regenerated plant. **Photograph 6.8.**

CHAPTER SEVEN

INITIAL REGROWTH

Once your plant has been successfully rescued, continue to water and feed as you would during a typical vegetative period—gradually increasing the nutrients until reaching her full requirements. The first grow (prior to the regeneration at hand) will have taught you her specific needs and tolerances. Now's the time to implement what you've learned.

Another activity that kept your plant busy during her initial grow (prior to harvest) was sturdy root development. She may need to be repotted. If you decide to increase her real estate, do it carefully—gently fluffing the root ball and trimming away any browned-off bits.

Importantly, never attempt to repot a plant prior to signs of regrowth. This places way too much stress on the plant. Always allow the plant to come back to life—expressing new growth—before you repot. If you do go this route, use the deepest pot you can. This is especially important if you want to regenerate your plant through several harvest cycles.

Curiously, the first foliage to appear at re-birth may be non-serrated, looking nothing like a regular-looking cannabis leaf at all, **photograph 7.1**. This is the plant's first line of action—the urgent deployment of solar panels (leaf matter) in order to gather light. Sometimes she'll forego the fancy, serrated design in order to do so. **Photograph 7.2** shows a whole flurry of these strange-looking emergency leaves. As growth continues and the plant stabilizes, these

7.1 A strange, non-serrated, emergency leaf.

7.2 Emergency leaves bursting forth, hungering for light.

7.3 The preferred staggered leaf set.

leaves will be followed by the more typical cannabis leaf. Some of the irregular leaves will, magically, morph into serrated leaves.

The new shoots will continue to develop in one of two possible growing configurations—each demanding specific treatment in order to maximize horizontal sprawl and the subsequent development of budding areas. How you treat this growth will be dependent on whether the fan leaves are developing opposite each other or in a staggered formation. These telltale characteristics will become obvious once the growing tips have reached about three to five inches in length, taking 10 to 14 days.

THE TREATMENT PROTOCOL FOR STAGGERED LEAF SETS

Staggered leaf sets are the preferred growing configuration. Fortunately, buds that flurry tend to produce this desired attribute. **Photograph 7.3** shows a typical staggered leaf formation. At each point where a leaf joins the main stem, a budding site will form. You can see this new growth in the photograph. Each growing stem will produce between four and eight budding sites as it is trained out towards

Figure 4. Bud Map (overhead plan) of staggered growth tips grown towards rim of 12-inch pot.

the edge of the pot. **Figure 4** is a plan from above—what I call a Bud Map—displaying how two buds (each with four growing shoots) can be trained horizontally, filling a 12-inch pot.

THE TREATMENT PROTOCOL FOR OPPOSING LEAF SETS

New growing stems with leaves appearing opposite each other, **photograph 7.4**, are not the preferred growing configuration. Buds that elongate after stabilization tend to produce this less desirable growth pattern. You may encounter either configuration, or sometimes a combination of both. You should encourage flurry wherever possible.

Growing stems, with leaves opposing each other, will be tipped—forcing the branch to split into two growing shoots. This process

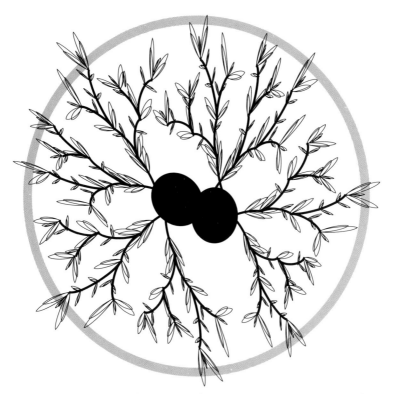

Figure 5. Bud Map (overhead plan) of tipped growth tips grown towards rim of 12-inch pot.

must only be applied once two pairs of shade leaves have grown along the shoot. Never before, or the tip will just continue where it left off—recovering, and then growing back as a single shoot. That's time and energy wasted. Properly applied, the process doubles the plant's yield potential (assuming it is applied to all growing tips simultaneously).

To tip a growing shoot, firstly expose the extreme apex of the new growth. Do this by gently bending the surrounding leaves downwards, out of the way, **photograph 7.5**. This exposes the tiny, flame-shaped-bundle of green that would, if left alone, grow into the next set of leaves. With tweezers, grab this nub at its base and gently pull it free. Do this cleanly by squeezing the tweezers, clipping right through the soft plant matter. In a week or so, you'll have two new growing shoots forming at this tipped point.[1] **Photograph 7.6**.

7.4 An opposing leaf set.

7.5 The newly exposed growth tip about to be pinched free.

7.6 Two new shoots appear at the previously tipped point.

Later, having allowed a week or two for these two new shoots to re-cover—and for them to each develop their own two sets of opposing leaves—you may repeat the tipping process. This will again (potentially) double the quantity of growing tips. **Figure 5** is a Bud Map, displaying how two buds (each with four growing shoots) can be tipped and trained horizontally, thus filling a 12-inch pot. In this Bud Map, each growing stem has been tipped twice to achieve the desired coverage. (You cannot tip forever. Remember the ceiling of potential? It also applies here, each plant having a genetic limit for this.)

CHAPTER EIGHT

STAKING, TEASING & TRAINING PRIOR TO FLOWERING

Continuing to use our 12-inch pot as an example, and assuming the regenerating stump to be centralized, it becomes clear that any particular tip need only be trained about six inches before reaching the pot's edge. Once the pot's rim is reached, the plant's growing shoots can only grow upwards, towards the light source. It will be our aim to pin down the growing shoots into a horizontal mat, reaching the edges of the pot over a three to five week period. The only piece of critical timing is in regards to when we switch the plant to a 12/12 light cycle to initiate flowering. But more on that later. For now, grab your pack of prepared stakes.

STAKING

The previously rescued (and capped) plant is now 15 days out from rebirth, and showing a flurry of sufficiently developed growing tips, many between one to three inches in length, ready for training, **photograph 8.1**.

Proceed by taking a single grow tip gently between fingers and thumb. Carefully bend it over, forming a nice curve. The young stem will be very flexible so don't fear breaking it, but don't force it either. Aim the stem towards the nearest edge of the pot. Then insert a stake immediately beside the stem, well towards the growing tip. Push the stake down into the pot carefully, being particularly sensitive to the huge root ball buried just below the surface. The MRS stakes are conceived to shimmy between roots rather than ripping through them—

8.1 An abundance of flurry, ready for training.

8.2 A flurried growth tip is gently bent over and secured by hooking the wire tie over it.

8.3 As the tip continues to grow towards the rim, additional stakes keep it horizontal.

8.4 Several stakes will be required to complete the journey. Be sure not to compromise the fresh nodal growth.

a good thing. Push the stake far enough into the pot so that you can firmly anchor the grow tip with the wire hook, forcing the branch to lie horizontally **(Photograph 8.2)**. The growing stem is secured by bending the stake's wire over the stem, immediately behind the growing mass. Just hook it in place. Don't tie her down (wrapping the wire around and around the branch) or you'll encounter trouble during harvest. If you think that the particular branch in question needs another stake to hold it, then don't be shy, **(Photographs 8.3 and 8.4)**. Just be sure that each stake goes behind a node so as not to obstruct growth. The developing plant will stiffen as it matures and this can push the stake(s) upward. To oppose this flexing of the plant's branches, insert the stakes at an angle. Aim each at an imaginary spot, midpoint, beneath the root ball. This angled insertion creates a natural brake, holding the stake firmly in place.

8.5 Twelve growing tips secured by stakes.

Repeat the staking process with each of the available (and sufficiently mature) growing shoots, pointing each towards the outer rim of the pot. **Photograph 8.5** displays 12 pinned shoots on our demonstration plant. Be aware that new growth will continue to develop from the centralized stump, and you should anticipate how you'll incorporate this into your horizontal spread. You will use many, many stakes in order to pin out an entire plant. Count on between 60 and 100 for a typical 12-inch pot.

 TEASING AND TRAINING

Remember the aim of the exercise? We are trying to create a flat top to present an efficient grow surface to our light. To maintain this, adjust the height of the stakes, keeping the top surface level, and the growing tips heading for the rim. Stake any new shoots as they appear.

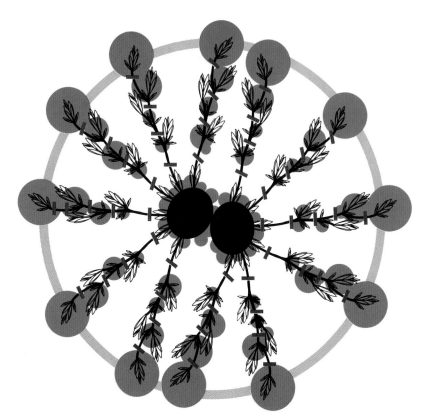

Figure 6. Bud Map (overhead plan) of staggered growth tips grown towards rim of 12-inch pot. Red dashes represent The MRS stakes and green dots represent buds of various yields. (Larger dots equal larger buds.) This Bud Map allows us to see how the stakes are positioned, and how bud formation can be expected to develop.

This ability to adjust height, maintaining a flat canopy, is a cornerstone element of The MRS.

Consider **figures 6 & 7**. We've encountered these previously in a simplified format. This time, however, I've overlaid further information—red dashes (representing The MRS stakes), and green dots (representing buds of various yields. Larger dots equal larger buds). This Bud Map allows us to see how the stakes are positioned, and how bud formation can be expected to develop. What may come as a surprise is the large number of stakes used. Aren't you glad you made a solid batch to begin with? Also, notice how the green dots are the largest around the pot's circumference. This indicates where the biggest, heaviest and

Figure 7. Bud Map (overhead plan) of tipped growth tips grown towards rim of 12-inch pot. Red dashes represent The MRS stakes and green dots represent buds of various yields. (Larger dots equal larger buds.) This Bud Map allows us to see how the stakes are positioned, and how bud formation can be expected to develop.

tastiest buds will form. There are two reasons for this. Firstly, these are the terminal shoots; the primary growing shoots at the ends of the main branches. Secondly, the position of these budding sites (around the outer edge of the pot) means they gather more available light. With the process of regeneration, we are presented with many colas—all scattered around the perimeter—all fighting for dominance. The outer buds will want to grow taller, giving the flat top a cratered look. Tame them the best you can by pushing the stakes a little deeper as needed.

The smaller dots in the illustrations show expected secondary bud formation. These are second and third node flower clusters that will, during maturity, reach upwards and become full-on buds of note.

8.6 Many secondary budding locations, spread along a single growth shoot.

8.7 The same budding locations, five weeks into flowering.

8.8 The beginnings of a regenerative vegetation period in a large 15-inch by 30-inch tub.

8.9 The rapid growth, three weeks later. Time to put the MRS stakes to use, spreading this foliage out.

Photograph 8.6 shows one branch that's been trained out to the edge of a large tub. Note the many potential budding points along its length. **Photograph 8.7** is the same branch, five weeks into flowering. These secondary buds will continue to develop and grow upwards towards the light.

It will become apparent as you work the growing tips outwards—in a horizontal plane—that a sort of acceleration has kicked in. You'll be going through stakes at a high speed and the plant will become very bushy. As an example of this prolific growth, and the lessons we've learned, look at **photographs 8.8 to 8.12**. These depict a plant growing in a 15-inch by 30-inch tub. The time taken to achieve the lovely flat top in **photograph 8.12** was just over five weeks. Note the staking procedure and the proliferation of stakes. Such an extreme rate of growth creates an abundance of leaf, much of which can create congestion, harboring moisture and pests. So keep your plant well ventilated, combing her daily with your outstretched fingers, **photograph 8.13**.

8.10 Training the still growing tips towards the outer rim of the grow tub.

8.11 The MRS at work. Her army of bamboo soldiers pinning down the solid and even flat top.

8.12 The results: a massive and well-vegetated plant, ready for the flowering cycle.

8.13 Grooming or combing the foliage with the fingers–on the lookout for pests, disease, and humidity problems.

CHAPTER NINE

THE SECOND FLOWERING

There are two rules that must be kept in mind as you prepare to begin the flowering cycle—your plant's second one. Balanced against each other, yin and yang-style, they define the plant's subsequent perform- ance under the imposed conditions. Here are the rules we must bring into harmony:

1. Switch to 12/12 just as the trained tips are about to reach the pot's outer rim.
2. Switch to 12/12 only if the plant has had a minimum of four to five weeks regeneration time.

When combined, the rules simply mean that you should switch to the 12/12 flowering cycle at least four to five weeks after the initial rescue and just before the growing tips reach the pot's outer rim. Quite a balancing act, although the timing required is actually easier to implement than it may seem at first. For example, the first week of the regeneration will be taken up with stabilization and waiting for signs of new growth. It's then going to take another week (or 10 days) for the new shoots to reach the proper size for training. So you are a good two to three weeks into the procedure before you set sail for the rim. As long as you reach the rim after another two to three weeks growth, and not before, you'll be fine.

But why?

Why is it important for the plant to regrow for at least four to five weeks? And, what's so important about how we handle growth at the pot's rim? The answers are related and intertwined, colliding at a point I'll dub "the stretchmark".

STRETCH

Stretch is a strange behavior. It is the elongation of the plant that occurs immediately following the switch to the 12/12 flowering cycle. It's at this point, marked by the sudden change of the photoperiod, that the plant is literally forced to switch gears. She must abruptly shift from vegetative growth to flower development.

Outdoors, in a natural setting, this happens over a period of time as the photoperiod contracts slowly, across the seasons. The plant's hormones dance along, facilitating this process—gradually, seamlessly.

Indoors however, with the sudden deprivation of light, there is no warning. It's immediate and abrupt—rather like you or I going to sleep on a hot summer's evening only to wake the next morning, knee deep in winter. The adjustment takes a little time to organize, and it is during this period of hormonal rebalancing the plant will elongate or stretch. Little new growth appears leaf-wise, but she will stretch between nodes. Budding density is partly related to internodal spacing, so this is not a good thing. We want tight internodes, not widely spaced ones. The period of stretch is normally passed by week three of flowering, with buds now developing strongly.

Stretch manifests itself differently, depending upon strain and plant maturity. It has been noted that the problem is minimized if switching to 12/12 when the vegetating plant is sexually mature (showing pre-flowers) and not before.

Experience has borne this out with me, and it's why I insist on allowing a regenerating plant a minimum of five weeks growth. She'll be healthier, bushier and probably showing signs of pre-flowering. The 12/12 flip of the lights won't come as such a shock as she's partly ready. Flowering will occur almost immediately (within one to six days) and stretch, while not eliminated altogether, will be minimized.

There are differences between how stretch affects plants grown in traditional ways and plants that are regenerated with The MRS. A plant grown in an orthodox fashion exhibits stretch predominantly at the central growing stem(s). With the process of regeneration it is the exact opposite—with stretch affecting the outer buds. These are the terminal tips around the outer rim of the pot. (See the large green dots shown around the rims in **figures 6 & 7**.) This means that no matter what configuration or vessel you regenerate in—be it a circular pot, a square pot, or a rectangular one—you'll always be faced with the prospect of the outer buds growing too fast, obscuring the more centralized growth from light. This is why it is important to begin the flowering cycle just as the growing shoots are pinned at the rim of the pot; maybe even just before. The secret is to switch to 12/12 and let them begin flowering as they stretch over the rim. Don't, on the other hand, let the branches grow over the rim, and then switch to 12/12. In this scenario, you'll run the risk of overgrowing the outer buds, resulting in an unruly, crater-shaped canopy. Remember, once you reach the outer rim of the pot, the only way for the growing shoots to go is up, towards the light. Apart from being able to adjust the overall canopy height (flatness) via the stakes, you can no longer apply any horizontal influence. It may take you one or two grow cycles to get the timing down to correctly anticipate the stretch-mark.

Familiarity with your strain and a little practice are the keys to success. Understand that failing to perfectly hit this stretchmark will not, in itself, prevent you achieving a great regenerative grow. It simply means having a slight unruly-ness to deal with, that's all. You'll still score a stack of juicy buds.

Once the lights are switched to 12/12, your only real concern will be maintenance throughout the typical eight-week flowering period. This will consist of a degree of defoliation, ensuring light reaches deep into the canopy, and physically controlling the flat top configuration for maximum light exposure.

❄ DEFOLIATION

Defoliation—the systematic removal of leaf matter with the intention of enhancing growth or flowering—is a touchy subject with growers. Many are firmly opposed, insisting that every leaf has a purpose unless the plant decides to jettison it. For this school of thought, the

9.1 Removing a light-deprived leaf.

removal of any shade leaf, even one obscuring a budding site, is considered abusive. Others swear that additional light falling on newly revealed buds enhances production. Both arguments hold water, and should be approached with balance and common sense.

It is important to remember that the process of regeneration (via The MRS) is not regular by any means. It's a unique discipline presenting us with a specific problem (an abundance of lush foliage) making defoliation somewhat mandatory.

By the first week of the flowering cycle you'll certainly notice your plant has developed a healthy head of green plumage. She'll be choking on shade leaves. These are the big multi-fingered fellas with fat stalks and you'll find them hogging the canopy, preventing light penetration. It will be necessary to thin these out over time, allowing the light to push deeper.

Begin by "combing" the plant with your fingers, every day or so as previously described—improving air circulation, the exchange of moisture (respiration/humidity) and allowing you to keep an eye out for pests and disease. Also remove discolored and aged leaves **(photograph 9.1)**. Pinch off large fan leaves from beneath the canopy

9.2 If you can't see the hidden bud, your light source can't either.

9.3 A fan leaf has been removed, revealing the previously obscured bud.

9.4 A canopy in need of some light defoliation.

(and low on the sides) as these leaves no longer receive light.

Permit the plant to flower happily until week four. Patiently keep the top of the plant flat over these few weeks by adjusting the stakes up or down as required. Along the way, further defoliate so that any buds hidden by fan leaves are revealed to the light. **Photographs 9.2** and **9.3** demonstrate how an obscured bud is revealed to the light by removing a covering fan leaf.

In regards to regeneration, moderate defoliation seems the best way to achieve solid light penetration, maintaining a healthy flat top. Here's my timetable:

■ Vegetative period: I do not defoliate at all—unless required for pest/disease control. The fan leaves are, indeed, important during the vegetative stage—sucking up the light and churning out all the goodness required for healthy roots and general wellbeing.

■ Week 1 of flowering: I only perform basic defoliation (as already described).

■ Week 4 of flowering: I defoliate just enough to clear away all fan leaves that are obscuring secondary budding sites. I also clear away

9.5 The above canopy, defoliated. You see more of the buds, so does your light.

as many fan leaves as I can from beneath the canopy. If they are not receiving light, they can go. You'll find many have yellowed for this very reason: Light deprivation.

■ Week 7 of flowering: I like to begin my flush (rinsing the pots with copious amounts of water to remove salt and nutrient build up from the roots), having defoliation well out of the way by this time. So, during weeks five to seven, we return to basic house-keeping duties—maintaining the plant and canopy—preparing for the forthcoming harvest. The now defoliated canopy will allow deep light penetration for these all-important final weeks—the period when our buds put on the most weight.

Photographs 9.4 and **9.5** show a plant before and after defoliation. You can see how the canopy of the cleaned plant is more open to light. The buds also look bigger. A hard and fast rule: The more bud you can see, the greater the light penetration will be.

Photograph 9.6 is a side view of a small plant, in a tiny six-inch pot, trained to demonstrate the desired horizontal growth pattern.

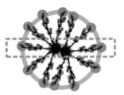

MAIN COLAS

SECONDARY BUDS

9.6 Side view of a small plant, in a tiny six-inch pot, trained to demonstrate the desired horizontal growth. Two weeks after harvesting and rescuing this plant, she presented 12 flurrying shoots. All but two were removed. This remaining pair aimed at opposite sides of the pot, and trained accordingly. Looking at the diagram accompanying the photograph, you can see I've suggested the pair of branches as being typical of that portioned off by the orange box: a cross-section. You'll notice that the buds at the very ends of the spread are the largest–as expected. The complete cross-section consists of these two main colas and eleven (visible) secondary buds spread between them. 13 growing buds in all, stretching up to seek the light, creating a flat top canopy.

Two weeks after harvesting and rescuing this plant, she presented 12 flurrying shoots. All but two were removed—the remaining pair aimed at opposite sides of the pot, and trained accordingly. Looking at the diagram accompanying the photograph, you can see I've suggested the pair of branches as being typical of that portioned off by the orange box: A cross-section. You'll notice that the buds at the very ends of the spread are the largest—as expected. The complete

9.7 Detail of how the small buds group to create the Double Ended Bud.

cross-section consists of these two main colas and eleven (visible) secondary buds spread between them. 13 growing buds in all, stretching up to seek the light, creating a flat top canopy. The full pot, if it had not had 10 growth tips removed to create the photograph, would have produced 70 or so great buds (6X13=78). This plant's buds would also have been considerably more substantial if the grow had been executed in a 12-inch pot with its greater capacity. The point of the exercise (and of me sacrificing all that potential bud for a photograph) is to visually drive home how we are attempting to horizontally pin down the branches, allowing the secondary buds to grow.

CHAPTER TEN

THE SECOND HARVEST

At this point, we have come full circle; beginning with a plant to be harvested, and now finishing in exactly the same position—with a plant to be harvested.

Two harvests, one plant. And, while she is technically the exact same plant as the one first encountered, she sure looks different with her flat top crop and supporting stakes. The pot should be bursting with good-sized buds, each ripe and fat **(Photograph 10.1)**.

Think back for a moment. It was only about three months ago that you last faced this plant at her crossover harvest. The sore toe has now healed, the nail is growing back just fine, and you made the right choice: Implementing The MRS. Power consumption has been minimized, making hardly a blip on your power bill. Nutrient and space requirements have been negligible. All you've really had to do is tend the plant, keeping her staked down and pest free. And, you're about to reap your second harvest—one bigger, plumper, and more fragrant than the first. Is this magic or what? Don't you wish it could be this way all the time?

Well, it can. Just as you had two choices with the initial harvest—either chop, hang and dump the stump; or chop, hang and regenerate the stump—you have the same two choices now. At this point, though, it's usually impossible to see the main trunk of the plant due to the forest of bamboo surrounding it. There is work to do: We need to remove all the supporting stakes before proceeding. No matter

10.1 Plump buds on the perimeter of a flat top grow.

10.2 Grasping a stake at its base.

10.3 Pushing the stake upwards.

10.4 As the stake is raised, the wire loop pops free.

10.5 The solid trunk of a regener- ated plant.

which course of action you decide upon (chop and hang or chop and regenerate) the initial preparation of the plant is the same: The removal of the stakes.[1] This should be an easy job, so long as you followed the staking instructions and only bent the wires over the branches, refraining from wrapping them. If you've done the proper thing, the stakes can be released by grasping them, one at a time, at their bases (**photograph 10.2**), and pushing upwards. In each instance, the top of the stake (wired end) should pop free, allowing it to be grasped and removed (**photographs 10.3 and 10.4**).

If you've not followed protocol, you'll need to plumb deep between the buds, uncurling the wires. If this is necessary, wear gloves. The sticky mess on your gloves is wasted resin (that could also have given you an unintended contact high). Lesson learned.

Once all of the stakes have been removed, the main trunk will be visible. You'll find it quite thick and stout due to the impressive load of bud and plant matter it has supported throughout the grow (**photograph 10.5**). You've created a mighty beast. It's now time to decide her future.

So, pick up those pruning shears.

What's it to be?

Chop and hang? Or do you want to go one more round, producing another chubby pot of buds?

PART THREE

ADVANCED TECHNIQUES

TECHNIQUES FOR SUCCESSIVE REGENERATIONS

REGENERATION TO COMPLEMENT CLONING AND SEEDING

EXPANDING THE MRS TO MULTIPLE PLANTS

CHAPTER ELEVEN

ADAPTING THE MRS FOR SUCCESSIVE REGENERATIONS

I didn't think you could resist.

I mean, why stop now?

You've learned how to rescue, regrow and re-flower your lovely cannabis plant, and the proof is before you. Continuing to another regeneration (and then another, and another) is a no brainer. To do so though, you must harvest a little differently.

Three months ago, at the cross-over harvest, it was easy to pinpoint and retain one or two buds for the regeneration process. With a regenerative harvest, it's not quite as simple. The branching, trained into the growth pattern, complicates matters. Bud is abundant deep inside the growth, hugging the main trunk.

Another problem presents itself. A regenerative harvest requires multiple chopping of branches, so there will be more than one severed appendage requiring rescue. Sealing multiple cuts with duct tape is not practical under these circumstances, so we'll call on the services of our trusty hot glue gun. Globs of molten glue are perfect for sealing the plant's open wounds. They are sterile, forming quickly with precision. So, heat up your gun and grab your garden pruners; let's get to work.

 SEALING THE CUT WITH GLUE

Begin by stretching out an individual branch **(photograph 11.1)**. Then cut it off, leaving the lowermost bud behind. This branch can be hung

11.1 A branch with several buds–ready to be cut from a regenerated plant, and hung to dry.

11.2 Trimming off individual buds–working in towards the center of the plant.

11.3 Having trimmed away the buds, a bonsai-like trunk—and a few straggling baby buds—is all that remains. These buds can, once again, be regenerated. Note the globs of white glue sealing the severed branches.

to dry. Immediately seal the exposed cut with a glob of glue from the glue gun. Simply squeeze out a nice glob. Do it quickly, before a bead of moisture appears over the cut making it tricky to achieve adhesion. Continue to trim the branches and individual buds from the plant **(photograph 11.2)**. In each instance, leave the branch's lowermost bud intact on the plant. Seal every cut as you proceed.

You'll finish with a very strange, bonsai-looking stump **(photograph 11.3)**. Yield-wise, a nice bunch of branches are hung and a pile of individual buds will need attention **(photograph 11.4)**.

Firstly, before attending your bounty, ensure your plant has every open wound properly capped with glue. Then gently trim the remaining buds, giving them a haircut as previously taught and shown in **photograph 11.5**. Feed her with a nice mild nutrient solution, **photograph 11.6**, and return her to continuous light. Within two weeks she'll flurry once more, **photograph 11.7**. After another four to five weeks, she'll be crawling over the pot's rim, ready to flower again.

The magical thing is that you can regenerate over and over again.

11.4 A handful of harvested, regenerated, buds.

11.5 Trimming a bud to encourage flurry during regeneration.

11.6 Watering a just rescued plant with a mild solution of nutrients.

11.7 After 14 days the remaining buds have flurried.

In due course, the regenerative plant will probably lose vigor; it's just natural. Recall the ceiling of potential? I'd imagine it applies here, although I've regenerated a plant a dozen times without any loss of quality, and I can't report ever seeing any deterioration or drop-off in vigor. I'm normally a tad weary of a particular plant long before loss of vigor is encountered.

A neat way to dry the individual buds harvested from a regenerated plant is something called necklacing. The procedure allows for controlled drying without inflicting ugly flat sides on the buds—something that occurs when you dry buds (laying flat) in a bag or box.

To necklace your buds, firstly manicure the sugar leaves. If you're a hash-maker, place them to one side—they'll make great hash. Now, position all the manicured buds side by side and estimate the total width. Then add 30%. For example, if you have 24 inches' worth of buds, add another eight inches, arriving at a total of 32 inches. Grab a roll of the gardening wire, the kind we used to originally make The MRS stakes. Cut off a length equal to the summed total. Thread the buds onto the wire carefully **(photographs 11.8** and **11.9)**. Continue

11.8 Poking a garden wire through a bud.

11.9 Slide the threaded buds along the wire to create a necklace.

11.10 The ends of the wire are brought together and fashioned into a rough hook.

11.11 Bud necklace can be hung where convenient, allowing buds to dry.

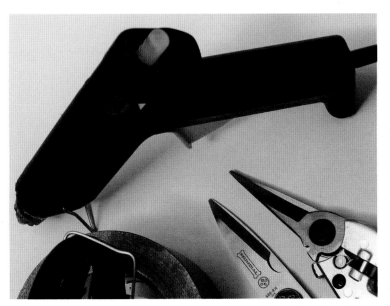

11.12 A glue gun is an essential tool, making the sealing of cut branches easy and efficient.

to thread all the buds in the same manner. When finished, twist and form the loose ends of wire into a rough hook **(photograph 11.10)**. This can be hung in a convenient place, allowing the buds to dry **(photograph 11.11)**. They shrink slightly during this, contracting away from each other. No flat sides. Trimming the sugar leaves and threading the buds will create sticky fingers. Scrape the resin off with a blade, adding it to any scissor hash that's been collected.

CHAPTER TWELVE

USING REGENERATION TO COMPLEMENT CLONING AND SEEDING

Now that we have the basics of regeneration under our belts, it's time to consider how the process can interface with the more familiar routes of propagation: Seed and clone. After all, there would be no cannabis plants at all if not for seed, and cloning (propagating from cuttings) is necessary for ensuring strain retention and for rapidly expanding a garden's size and output.

The rapid growth offered by a regenerating plant, combined with the multiple bud output of The MRS, offer useful enhancements in both areas.

✺ HOW REGENERATION CAN COMPLEMENT CLONING

Cloning is the process of taking cuttings from a vegetating plant and regrowing these into full-sized duplicates of the original **(photograph 12.1)**. Gardeners and farmers have been doing this for thousands of years. One plant can become two plants, three or even a field full of green. As the genetics of each plant remain identical to the donor (mother) plant, cloning allows refinement and conservation of genetics. Poor plants can be weeded out and only the best plants cloned to replace them.

12.1 An array of cloned plants, labeled.

The MRS allows us to create a strong and densely populated mother plant for clone harvesting. We just need to tweak the usual regenerative procedure a little. Here are two approaches: stumpy style and traditional.

STUMPY STYLE CLONING FROM A REGENERATED PLANT

Normally, one clones from the young, healthy, and succulent growing shoots on a vegetating plant. This is the traditional way, and it can allow the taking of 10, 20 or many more cuttings at one time. It's something we'll look at a little later. The stumpy style is different and entails the culling of stump ends from a plant that has been regenerated at least once. It's a handy technique for when you require a small number of clones. The method is a time saver: You don't need to grow out the vegetation before taking the cuttings, working instead with the first signs of growth.

The plant shown in **photograph 12.2** is one we harvested earlier in the book. Note the multiple wound treatments in the form of glue globs and the aged duct tape. This plant would normally be regenerated by

12.2 A just harvested, previously regenerated stump.

12.3 After two weeks the stump has regrown fresh leaves.

12.4 Tools required for cloning.

trimming the remaining buds to encourage flurry, and returning her to a 24/0 light regime. However, for the purposes of stumpy cloning, we don't require a flurry, so we can skip the bud trimming. Otherwise, we'll treat her exactly as if we're regenerating; she receives a nice bath of nutrients before returning to the continuous light. In a week or two, the buds will show elongation and new leaves **(photograph 12.3)**. She is now ready to donate her growing tips.

Photograph 12.4 shows us the tools we require for cloning. These are:

■ Scissors: I like good quality kitchen scissors. Made with stainless steel blades, they somehow feel clean and hygienic. Good for surgery. Traditional wisdom suggests a razor blade is better suited to the task, but we're dealing with branches here—woody and tough. Whatever your tool of choice, be sure it's sterile.

■ Glass of water: Preferably distilled, but bottled will be fine. You'll be dipping the cut branches into this water immediately after chopping them from the plant.

■ Rooting powder or gel: Available from your garden supply store,

12.5 Poking holes in growing medium with a pen.

this is a hormonal growth enhancer, normally powered with Thiamine. Never work straight from the original container; always pour what you need into a separate vessel, avoiding any possibility of back contamination. If using the powdered version, a face mask is also a good idea. (Unless, of course, you want to develop hairy palms. Only joking.)

■ Small pots: These can be individual pots or a poly-tray consisting of many little cups. Just ensure they have proper drainage.

Begin by filling the pots with your preferred grow medium (for me, that's perlite) and soaking with a diluted nutrient mix. Once the excess has drained off, poke a hole (an inch or so deep) into the middle of each receptacle. Use a pen or stick **(photograph 12.5)**.

Returning to our donor plant and her new growth, consider appropriate branches to target. Look for strong and knobby ones, topped with lush new growth. **Photograph 12.6** shows five suitable branches cut from the plant. Each consists of a good length of woody matter below the nub of growth. Drop the branches into the glass of water immediately after you cut them from the plant. They can rest

12.6 Target branches cut from the regenerating stump.

here for the time being, safe from the danger of embolism, as you continue examining them individually. These branches are not yet ready to be treated with rooting powder, or to be potted, as a second (and very specific) cut is needed for each. So grab your scissors and position the rooting powder (or gel) nearby.

Over the decades I've had little luck with cloning, experiencing high failure rates. No matter how carefully I followed instructions gleaned from books and magazines, I'd see barely 20% of the cuttings through the first week or two. One day I stumbled across the idea of leaving a little stumpy matter behind, and that seemed to solve the problem. Using this idea, which I'm sure many others have also discovered for themselves, I now approach a 90% success rate.

Examine the branch in **photograph 12.7**. Note the knobs and bumps along the woody stem. All of these represent a little twist, turn, sprout or nub that has been active with growth at some point in the past. Retaining a little tiny piece of this at the point of the second cut seems to create prompt root growth. **Photograph 12.8** shows where I've decided to apply this second cut, and you can see the little bump where a secondary branch once forked away.

12.7 Detail of knobby branch with possible locations for second cut.

12.8 The branch is cut retaining a knobby portion of branch to improve rooting.

12.9 Having been dipped in rooting powder, the branch is potted.

Dip the newly cut branch into the water, followed by the rooting powder, coating it thickly with the stimulating hormone. Then, being careful not to scrape off the accelerant, insert the prepared branch into one of your propagation pots **(photograph 12.9)**. Gently tamp it down making sure it is secure.

Repeat with all cuttings.

To stimulate the production of roots, place the cuttings under continuous, gentle, fluorescent light, leaving them undisturbed for a week to 10 days. (Spray gently with distilled water during this period to keep the potting material moist.) A successfully rooted branch can be seen in **photograph 12.10**. Repotted in a larger receptacle **(photograph 12.11)**, it will grow into a full and healthy plant, genetically identical to its mother.

TRADITIONAL CLONING FROM A REGENERATED PLANT

Typically, clones are taken from a healthy and lush plant with many growing branches. Such a plant is known as a mother, and she can deliver dozens of shoots for cloning. We have seen that regeneration

12.10 Root growth after a week or two under gentle fluorescent lights (24/0).

12.11 The now rooted clone is repotted in a more substantial pot where she will grow as a genetic duplicate of her mother.

12.12 A flurried plant without The MRS being applied to hold her branches horizontally. Grown like this she presents many shoots for cloning.

12.13 A typical shoot suitable for cloning.

can produce abundant and very quick growth, and it's something that we've been staking down with The MRS up until this point. By altering our tactics—that is, not staking out the flurrying growth—we can create a wonderful clone mother instead of an ordered flat top. **Photograph 12.12** shows such a plant and **photograph 12.13** displays one of the many resulting donor branches.

Take your cuttings along the branches, midway between leaf sets **(photographs 12.14** and **12.15)**. Rest the cuttings in water immediately after they are removed from the plant **(photograph 12.16)**.

You now need to dress each branch, in turn, with a final cut. Unlike the stumpy clone procedure, where you cut at a nub, this time you'll need to actually create a grow nub. Do this by carefully trimming away the first leaf above the initial cut, leaving its base (the very point it joins the branch) intact **(photograph 12.17)**. This spot of previous growth activity, if left as described, increases the chances of successful rooting. Dip the branch into water, followed by the rooting solution, before planting into the propagation mix. Repeat with all cuttings to fill your tray. Place the clones under continuous and gentle light **(photograph 16.18)**. They'll reshoot within two weeks, each becoming a new plant, each identical to its mother.

12.14 A shoot cut from a branch, ready to be cloned. Note the leaf low on the shoot. This will be partially removed, leaving a nub to encourage root growth.

12.15 The position on the mother plant where the cutting was taken. The healthy nub at the point below will rapidly re-grow over the ensuing weeks.

As an added bonus, the mother plant will quickly recover, sending up new shoots from the nodes immediately below the cut points **(photographs 12.19** and **12.20)**. These can be harvested for additional cloning or the mother plant can be allowed to flower.

HOW REGENERATION CAN COMPLEMENT SEED MANUFACTURE

Seeds are magic. Amazing little time capsules. Each encloses, safeguards and cradles thousands of years' worth of refined genetics. Creating your own seeds, your own plants, your own strains is wonderful, and something open to anyone who wants to put in the effort. I've listed reference material at the back of this book if you'd like to more fully explore the subject. What concerns us here is how the process of regeneration can be applied.

12.16 Cuttings resting in a glass of water awaiting their final dressing prior to repotting.

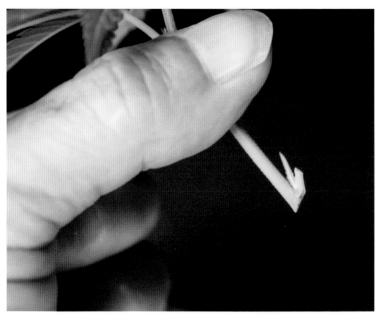

12.17 The lower leaf has been trimmed from the cutting leaving a nub.

12.18 Tray of clones under gentle fluorescent light.

12.19 Detail of cut branch on mother plant and the spot at which she will regrow.

Pollinating a female cannabis plant is as easy as leaving a mature male nearby. The pollen is fine, a single waft can fertilize an entire grow room. That's the easy way. However, breeders of cannabis love the fact that the females are, one could say, promiscuous. It is possible to pollinate multiple buds (on the same plant) with multiple males, producing multiple and completely unique sets of seeds. This is called selective pollination, and, this is where The MRS comes in— her buds, being plentiful and consistent in size, make perfect seed banks. If you wanted to, you could fertilize an entire flat top canopy with as many as 30 or more separate, individual, males. This is the opportunity afforded by The MRS.

The use of water as a neutralizing agent, in combination with little absorbent paper cones, is how I control a multi-donor fertilization— producing several unique hybrids from one female.

Cannabis flowers are best pollinated when they are between two and three weeks old. The clusters of young buds in **photograph 12.21** are the correct age. In addition to your cache of pollen and applicator brushes, you will need some paper towels (the kind used

12.20 Vigorous regrowth of the mother plant's previously severed branch.

12.21 Buds, two to three weeks old, perfect for pollinating to produce seeds.

12.22 Cornucopia wrapped around target buds. A paper funnel protects against pollinating adjacent buds.

12.23 Buds, in their protective cone, ready to be fertilized with a soft brush.

in the kitchen to wipe up spills), a water bottle (spray type) filled with tap water and a roll of adhesive tape.

You'll need the pollen from a male cannabis plant. I'll assume that you have either a male that's come into flower, or that you've stored a sample (shaken from its flowers and then sealed in an airtight container) in the freezer. Pollen can be stored for up to three months this way.

Back to the females: Select the young buds you wish to fertilize, and a corresponding number of napkin squares. Form a cornucopia, with a single square of napkin, around each target bud. This is much like wrapping a bunch of flowers for a loved one. You are enclosing the bud in a cone of absorbent and translucent paper, affixing it with a piece of adhesive tape **(photograph 12.22)**. You'll note the cone remains open at the top, allowing access to the targeted floral clusters **(photograph 12.23)**. Repeat with all the target buds.

With the water bottle, spray all the buds you do not wish to fertilize. The idea is to soak them with water so that they immediately reject

12.24 A successfully fertilized bud showing seeds at its crown.

any pollen that may spill. Using your free hand as a shield, protect your target buds from overspray.

You may now carefully apply previously collected pollen to the target buds. When done, gently fold over the tops of the cones and seal them shut with another piece of tape. With the fertilized buds sealed within their translucent cones, return the plant to its flowering light cycle (12/12).

After two days, re-douse the plant with water. This time, soak the paper cones too. Get everything nice and wet, stopping any still-viable pollen in its tracks. The sodden cones will now easily peel away from the fertilized buds.

Allow the seeds to form and ripen for at least four weeks. Six weeks is preferable if you can manage it. Mature seeds always have a superior germination rate. You want them rattling in their pods, so to speak. **Photograph 12.24** is a successfully fertilized bud with young seeds forming at the crown.

CHAPTER THIRTEEN

EXPANDING THE MRS TO MULTIPLE PLANTS

The MRS was designed as a stand-alone system built around a single 12-inch pot and a single cost-effective LED light. However, if you have a light capable of growing a square meter (3.5 x 3.5 feet) of plants, then there are two ways you can upscale The MRS to take advantage of the lumens. You can either upscale with clones, or via the successive regeneration of a single plant in an oversized grow box.

By taking clones, you can grow nine plants (each in its own 12-inch pot), harvesting and regenerating them, with the pots in a square (3-pot by 3-pot) grid. That's approximately five hundred colas, under one light, in nine manageable pots. The grid creates an area one-meter square, perfect for a small grow room and a medium sized LED light. A modular approach like this is easy to handle and to size according to need. For instance, a 2-pot by 2-pot array forms a nice stepping stone, allowing you to test the waters of expansion. Its combined flat top will span about 24 inches, perfect for a small/medium LED grow light to handle.

The only downside of this modular approach is waste, or more precisely, wasted potential. Consider **figure 8**. This shows our grid of pots; the area in white is the wasted space between them. All up, about 20% of the available grow space is lost. Translated, that's about one hundred buds worth of lost yield for each subsequent harvest.

A superior approach is to use a custom grow box, one that's a meter square in size. You can locate these at the big gardening stores, sold as self-contained vegetable beds, complete with legs and rollers.

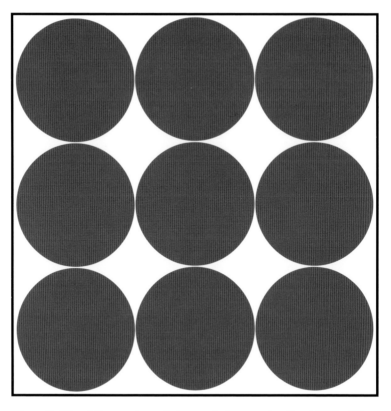

Figure 8. The white area is wasted space between pots. About 20% of the available grow space is lost. Translated to colas, that's 100 extra colas we could have grown if using a single grow box, rather than a grid of pots.

A wonderful book about container growing is *True Living Organics* by The Rev, (Green Candy Press, 2012). I'd suggest grabbing this book; it's a goldmine of relevant information. You can populate this square meter of space by using The MRS in either of two ways:

■ Centre a single plant, and over two or three regenerations stake her out to fill the space, or
■ Plant nine regenerated clones as a grid into the larger space.

The latter method is faster, as you're populating from nine starting places simultaneously. Thus, the many plants fill in the gaps promptly. However, it is a quick fix. The first method is actually preferred, even

13.1 Container grow producing masses of young bud.

though it's a lot more work. This is because the root ball can be allowed to develop naturally without having to fight its neighbors. The payoff is *additional* and healthy regenerative cycles—more cycles than is possible if nine plants are fighting for room.

Starting with a single pot (60 colas) it is possible, across three regenerative cycles, to fill out a grow box one-meter square. You can then generate over 600 colas with each regenerative cycle. And you'll have enjoyed hundreds of great buds along the way.

FINAL WORDS

Books and cannabis share a unique property. They are both capable of creating transcendence for the user. We can smoke some heavenly sativa and be swept away; seeing things, hearing sounds, tasting flavors, all in new ways, and with fresh insight. If we can then bring the new insight back, to our everyday realities, we have achieved transcendence. Mystics, shamans, medicine men, poets, artists, and mere mortals, have been accessing this special place—in search of transcendence—since the evolution of thought (and the ability to imagine) emerged as human functions. And it's no mere illusion, either. Personally, I struggled for years trying to fully appreciate the implications of Einstein's famous equation $E=MC^2$. I just couldn't quite get my head around it. A lovely sativa called Neville's Haze solved the problem. It became blindingly clear, and I managed to "bring it back."

Likewise, a book can change the way we perceive our world, often allowing us to see and understand concepts and ideas in ways not considered before. We can become lost in the book, absorbing new and interesting minutiae, and then "bring the information back"—putting it to use.

As an example, this book began with some fairly unusual propositions. Statements and claims you probably read with a certain level of skepticism, a certain degree of doubt. I understand. But now—having digested the book—I hope you'll read the very same words with excitement and wonder. And, that's transcendence.

FOOTNOTES

INTRODUCTION

1. It was not so wonderful the following day when Ricky showed up, baggie in hand and an excited look in his eye, only to hear that Billie had popped my cannabis cherry. Life is full of surprises.

2. Although it had been an open secret for decades, the true identity of Mr. X was confirmed to author Keay Davidson, in 1999, during an interview with Dr. Lester Grinspoon.

3. Jack Herer interviewed by Steven Hager (*High Times*, April, 1990).

CHAPTER ONE: CONCEPTUALLY SPEAKING

1. This oddity is explained in Chapter 9, **photograph 9.6**. By chopping off the complete horizontal span, at the trunk's apex, you'll be left with what appears to be a double-ended bud. This makes a brilliant (and bizarre) gift for the stoner friend who thinks he's "seen it all."

2. This acronym (The MRS) is purposely cutesy and, I think, appropriate. We do, after all, worship our ladies. A successful grow is a marriage of sorts. It has to be.

CHAPTER THREE: INCREASED YIELD

1. One of the most remarkable tricks of the female cannabis plant is the production of a small bundle of male flowers for—you guessed it—self-fertilization. This evolved mechanism is sometimes triggered if a flowering female is allowed to run a couple of weeks past maturation, without being introduced to a friendly male. *I'll do it myself*, she seems to decide.

2. *SOG* stands for *Sea Of Green* and entails planting dozens of plants in extreme proximity. Side growth is minimized by this, and the plants grow as a sea of single main colas. *SCROG* is similar except it uses a screen of mesh laid over the plants. Growing tips are allowed to pass through the screen while other foliage is held back below the screen. The end result is, again, a sea of growing tips in close proximity. Both systems aim to create the coveted *flat top* for light-capturing efficiency.

CHAPTER FOUR: SAVING LIGHT, POWER SPACE AND CONSUMABLES

1. *HGL Technologies, LLC.* website: http://hydrogrowled.com

2. The Tardis is the famed "police box" time machine from the *BBC* series *Doctor Who.*

CHAPTER SIX: RESCUING AND REGENERATING YOUR HARVESTED PLANT

1. A plant's vascular system can (roughly) be compared to an animal's cardiovascular system. However, unlike the arteries, veins and mechanical hearts (found in we with legs), plants are plumbed with lignified tissues (xylem) for conducting water and minerals throughout. The fluids are drawn (from the roots, up the trunk and into the branches and leaves) by capillary action—a neat trick using the surface tension of water.

CHAPTER SEVEN: INITIAL REGROWTH

1. If you are clumsy, leaving ragged bits behind, you are technically *FIM-ing*. This can create a cluster of many new shoots. Great under normal circumstances, but not here, as we are aiming for the outer rim in an organized manner. By the way, *FIM* stands for *Fuck I Missed*. I kid you not.

CHAPTER TEN: THE SECOND HARVEST

1. The MRS stakes can be saved and reused for your next regenerative grow. Soak them overnight in a 10% solution of hydrogen peroxide, then allow them to dry in the sun. This kills off any nasties.

FURTHER READING

- *A Child's Garden of Grass*, by Jack S. Margolis and Richard Clorefene, Pocket Books, 1976
- *Cannabis Cultivation*, 3rd edition, by Mel Thomas, Green Candy Press, 2012
- *Cannabis Cultivator*, by Jeff Ditchfield, Green Candy Press, 2009
- *Cannabis: Evolution and Ethnobotany*, by Robert C. Clarke and Mark D. Merlin, University of California Press, 2013
- *Cannabis: The Genus Cannabis*, edited by David T. Brown, Harwood Academic Publishers, 1998
- *Carl Sagan: A Life*, by Keay Davidson, John Wiley & Sons, Inc., 1999
- *Cultivating Exceptional Cannabis*, by DJ Short, Quick American, 2003
- *Frankenstein; or, The Modern Prometheus*, by Mary Shelley, Lackington, Hughes, Harding, Mavor & Jones, 1818
- *Handbook of Cannabis Therapeutics*, edited by Ethan B. Russo, MD and Franjo Grotenhermen, MD, The Haworth Press, 2006
- *Marijuana Medicine*, by Christian Rätsch, Healing Arts Press, 2001
- *Marihuana Reconsidered*, by Lester Grinspoon, Harvard University Press, 1971
- *Organic Marijuana Soma Style*, by Soma, Quick American, 2005
- *The Cannabis Breeder's Bible*, by Greg Green, Green Candy Press, 2005
- *The Cannabis Grow Bible*, by Greg Green, Green Candy Press, 2003
- *The Hitchhiker's Guide to the Galaxy*, by Douglas Adams, Pan Books, 1979*
- *The Emperor Wears No Clothes*, by Jack Herer, HEMP Publishing, 1990
- *The Medical Cannabis Guidebook*, by Jeff Ditchfield and Mel Thomas, Green Candy Press, 2014
- *The Medicinal Uses of Cannabis and Cannabinoids*, edited by Geoffrey W Guy, Brian A Whittle and Philip J Robson, Pharmaceutical Press, 2004
- *True Living Organics*, by The Rev, Green Candy Press, 2012

* Without a doubt, one of the funniest and most profound books you can read, whether indulging the herb or not.

ABOUT THE AUTHOR

J.B. Haze is an innovative grower favoring "the dazzling magic of re-generation" over the more traditional methods of cultivation. A true hippy at heart—well traveled, well-toked, and insanely curious—J.B. Haze brings an educational, friendly, and humorous style of writing to the cannabis genre. He lives in a sunny corner of the antipodes with his cat and his guitars.

INDEX